CW00925518

Joachim and Anne

Love for Generations

Joachim and Anne
First century BC
Joachim was born in Nazareth
Anne was born in Bethlehem
Family connection: Grandparents

Text by Barbara Yoffie
Illustrated by Katherine A. Borgatti

Liguori

Dedication

To my family:
my parents Jim and Peg, my husband Bill, our son Sam
and daughter-in-law Erin, and our precious grandchildren
Ben, Lucas, and Andrew.

To all the children I have had the privilege of
teaching throughout the years.
And to grandparents who give witness and share their
faith and love of God with their grandchildren.

Imprimi Potest:
Harry Grile, CSsR, Provincial
Denver Province, the Redemptorists

Published by Liguori Publications
Liguori, Missouri 63057

To order, call 800-325-9521 or visit Liguori.org

p ISBN 978-0-7648-2292-6
e ISBN 978-0-7648-6911-2

Liguori Publications, a nonprofit corporation, is an apostolate of the Redemptorists.
To learn more about the Redemptorists, visit Redemptorists.com.

Printed in the United States of America
25 24 23 22 21 / 6 5 4 3 2
First Edition

Dear Parents and Teachers:

Saints and Me! is a series of children's books about saints, with six books in each set. The first set, *Saints of North America,* honors holy men and women who blessed and served the land we call home. The second set, *Saints of Christmas,* includes heavenly heroes who inspire us during Advent and Christmas and teach us to love the Infant Jesus.

Saints of Families introduces the virtuous lives of seven saints from different times and places who modeled God's love and charity within and for families. Saint Thérèse of Lisieux felt the love of her family and carried it into her religious community (which included her sisters). Saint Anthony of Padua is the patron of children, especially infants. Saint John Bosco cared for young, homeless boys, raising them like sons. Saint Thomas More, a father of four, imitated Christ's sacrificial love and devotion to the truth until death. Saints Joachim and Anne became the grandparents of Jesus, raising Mary as a sinless disciple. And Saint Gerard Majella, the patron of mothers, blessed families with food, knowledge, penances, and healing miracles.

Which saint stood up against a king? Who became a tailor and a lay brother? Which saint is "the Little Flower"? Who was known for his excellent preaching? Which saints lived before Jesus? Which saint climbed trees, did flips, and turned cartwheels? Find out in the *Saints of Families* set, part of the *Saints and Me!* series, and help children connect with the lives of saints.

Introduce your children or students to the *Saints and Me!* series as they:

—READ about the lives of the saints and are inspired by their stories.

—PRAY to the saints for their intercession.

—CELEBRATE the saints and relate to their lives.

John Bosco
1815–1888
Born: Becchi, Italy

Joachim and Anne
First century BC
Born: Nazareth (Joachim) Bethlehem (Anne)

Anthony of Padua
1195–1231
Born: Lisbon, Portugal

Gerard Majella
1726–1755
Born: Muro, Italy

Thérèse of Lisieux
1873–1897
Born: Alençon, France

Thomas More
1478–1535
Born: London, England

This is a story about two special saints: Joachim and Anne. They were the parents of Mary and the grandparents of Jesus. They loved Mary and their grandson, Jesus, very much.

Joachim and Anne lived a long time ago in Jerusalem. Joachim was a shepherd. He took care of sheep in the fields. His wife, Anne, took care of the house and the garden. Anne liked to cook, make bread, and sew clothing.

Joachim and Anne loved each other very much. Life was simple, and they were happy. They prayed every day and talked about God. Joachim and Anne helped the poor and gave them food to eat.

"We have everything we need," said Anne. "Yes, God has blessed us," Joachim answered. "I wish we had a baby like our friends," sighed Anne. Joachim hugged his wife and whispered, "Some day God will hear our prayers." Many years passed.

One day while Joachim was praying, an angel appeared to him. The angel said, "God has heard your prayers. You will soon have a very special baby to love."

Joachim was so surprised! He could hardly wait to tell Anne the good news.

Anne was in the garden. She was praying and saw an angel, too! The angel said, "You are going to have a special baby girl. She will be loved by many people." Anne ran off to find Joachim.

Joachim and Anne met at the city gate. They hugged each other. "I have wonderful news!" cried Anne. "So do I!" said Joachim. They thanked God for answering their prayers. After waiting many years, they were going to have a baby.

Anne gave birth to a beautiful baby girl. They named her Mary. Anne held Mary close and whispered, "God has a special plan for you, my little one." She kissed her and sang to her until she fell asleep.

Mary grew up in a holy and loving family. Joachim and Anne taught her how to love and serve God. They read Scripture together. Anne taught Mary songs and prayers. She showed her how to do simple chores.

Joachim and Anne took Mary to the Temple, where she learned more about God. "I like to listen to stories about God's people," Mary said. Mary's love for God grew every day.

Many years later, Mary became engaged to a man named Joseph. An angel appeared to her. "God loves you, Mary. You are going to have a baby boy. This is God's special plan for you," said the angel. Mary, pure and holy, was to become the Mother of Jesus!

Joachim and Anne had taught Mary to love and trust in God. Mary was ready to do what God asked of her. Joseph and Mary became the parents of Jesus, our Savior.

Joachim and Anne became grandparents the day Jesus was born. "Now we have a precious grandson to love," said Anne. Joachim and Anne were filled with joy.

Joachim and Anne shared the traditions of their faith with Jesus. They shared family stories from long ago. They taught him simple prayers. Joachim and Anne were wise and loving grandparents.

Jesus felt the warmth and love of his parents and grandparents. They passed their faith and love to Jesus and future generations. Even today we learn lessons of trust and hope from these two faithful saints, Joachim and Anne.

Each generation touches the next one. Let love for future generations begin in the heart of your family. You have so much to share about your faith!

Share your faith and let it show,
Pass on love and let it grow.

Dear god
I love you.

Saints Joachim and
Anne also loved you.

Bless my parents and
grandparents.
Keep us always
close to you.

Amen.

NEW WORDS (Glossary)

Angel: A spiritual being; God's helper and messenger

Engaged: One who has promised to marry another

Generation: A group of people born and living at the same time

Grandparent: The parent of a mother or father

Savior: The one who protects us from the dangers of evil; Jesus Christ

Shepherd: A person who takes care of sheep

Temple: A place of worship and learning for Jewish people

Traditions: Beliefs and ways of doing things that are passed down from parent to child

The Shrine of Sainte-Anne-de-Beaupré is a famous place to go to in Quebec City, Canada. It is dedicated to Saint Anne, the mother of Mary and grandmother of Jesus. It welcomes nearly one million visitors a year.